Unlocking Potential

Strategies for Maximizing Student Achievement and Engagement

Micky Wintringham

loss due to the information herein, either directly or indirectly. Respective authors own all copyrights not held by the publisher. The information herein is offered for informational purposes solely, and is universal as so. The presentation of the information is without contract or any type of guarantee assurance. The trademarks that are used are without any consent, and the publication of the trademark is without permission or backing by the trademark owner. All trademarks and brands within this book are for clarifying purposes only and are the owned by the owners themselves, not affiliated with this document.

Table of Contents

Chapter 1

Understanding Student Needs

Identifying Diverse Learning Styles

Every student enters the classroom with a unique set of experiences, preferences, and abilities. Recognizing these differences is crucial for educators who aim to create an inclusive and effective learning environment. Identifying diverse learning styles is the first step in tailoring instruction to meet the needs of each student.

Learning styles are generally categorized into visual, auditory, and kinesthetic modalities. Visual learners process information best when it is presented in a pictorial or graphic format. They benefit from diagrams, charts, and written directions. Auditory learners, on the other hand, prefer listening to explanations and discussions. They excel when information is presented through lectures, podcasts, or group conversations. Kinesthetic learners are hands-on and need to engage physically with the material to grasp concepts. They thrive in environments that allow them to use their bodies and manipulate objects.

Understanding these fundamental categories is essential, but it is equally important to recognize that students may not fit neatly into one single category. Many students exhibit a mix of these learning styles, and their preferences can change depending on the subject matter or context. Thus, a flexible and adaptive approach to teaching is necessary.

To identify students' learning styles, educators can employ a variety of methods. Observational strategies are effective in discerning how students interact with different types of content. For example, a teacher might notice that a particular student excels in tasks that involve reading and writing but struggles with oral instructions. This observation can hint at a strong visual learning preference. Similarly, a student who participates eagerly in discussions and recalls verbal instructions well may be an auditory learner. A kinesthetic learner might show a preference for lab experiments or physical activities over theoretical lessons.

Another useful tool is the implementation of learning style assessments or questionnaires. These instruments can provide insights into students' preferred learning modalities by asking questions about their study habits and preferences. While not definitive, these assessments can serve as a starting point for further exploration and discussion with students about their learning preferences.

It's also beneficial to engage students in conversations about their learning experiences. Asking students directly about what helps them learn best can yield valuable information. These discussions can help students become more aware of their own learning styles and advocate for their needs. Teachers can use this information to adjust their instructional strategies accordingly.

Recognizing diverse learning styles is not just about categorizing students; it's about understanding the rich tapestry of individual differences and how they impact learning. For instance, cultural background can influence learning preferences. In some cultures, oral traditions are strong, and students from such backgrounds may have a natural inclination toward auditory learning. Similarly, students with different socio-economic backgrounds might have varied experiences that shape their learning preferences.

Once learning styles are identified, the next step is to incorporate this knowledge into instructional practices. For visual learners, teachers can use visual aids such as charts, graphs, and images. Highlighting key information in different colors and using graphic organizers can also help these students process information more effectively. Incorporating videos and infographics can make abstract concepts more tangible.

For auditory learners, incorporating more verbal instruction into lessons can be beneficial. This might include reading aloud, using storytelling techniques, and engaging students in discussions and debates. Audiobooks and recordings can supplement traditional reading materials. Encouraging students to explain concepts in their own words or to teach peers can also reinforce their learning.

Kinesthetic learners benefit from hands-on activities and movement. Incorporating physical activities into lessons, such as experiments, building models, or using manipulatives, can help these students engage with the material. Allowing for movement in the classroom, such as standing desks or opportunities for students to move around, can also support their learning process. Role-playing and simulations can make learning more interactive and memorable for these students.

It's crucial to create a balanced instructional approach that incorporates elements for all learning styles. This not only ensures that all students have the opportunity to succeed but also exposes them to different ways of learning, which can be beneficial in developing a well-rounded skill set. For example, a lesson plan might start with a brief lecture (auditory), followed by a visual presentation of the key points (visual), and conclude with a hands-on activity (kinesthetic). This multimodal approach caters to different learning preferences and keeps students engaged.

Differentiation is another key strategy in addressing diverse learning styles. This involves tailoring instruction to meet the individual needs of students. Teachers can differentiate content, process, product, or learning environment based on students' learning styles. For instance, in a science class, while one group of students might be working on a lab experiment (kinesthetic), another group could be analyzing data through charts and graphs (visual), and a third group could be discussing their hypotheses and findings (auditory).

Technology can play a significant role in supporting diverse learning styles. Digital tools and resources offer a variety of ways to present information and engage students. Interactive simulations, educational games, and multimedia presentations can cater to different learning preferences. Online platforms can provide personalized learning experiences, allowing students to progress at their own pace and according to their preferred learning style.

However, it's important to avoid pigeonholing students into fixed categories. Learning styles should be seen as a framework for understanding how students prefer to learn, rather than rigid classifications. Encouraging students to develop flexibility in their learning approaches can help them become more adaptable and resilient learners. This involves exposing them to different types of learning experiences and teaching them strategies to tackle tasks that may not align with their preferred learning style.

Teachers must also be mindful of the potential for bias in identifying and addressing learning styles. It's essential to ensure that all students have equal access to different types of learning opportunities and that no group is favored over another. Regular reflection and feedback from students can help teachers adjust their practices to better meet the needs of all learners.

Recognizing Socio-Emotional Factors

Teachers often focus on academic content and instructional strategies, but recognizing socio-emotional factors is equally critical for maximizing student achievement and engagement. Students come to school with a wide array of emotional experiences and social backgrounds that profoundly influence their learning. Understanding these factors can help educators create a supportive environment that nurtures not only the intellect but also the emotional well-being of each student.

Children's socio-emotional development involves their ability to understand and manage their emotions, establish positive relationships, and make responsible decisions. These skills are essential for success in school and life. Emotional regulation, for example, allows students to cope with stress and persevere through challenges. Social skills enable them to collaborate effectively with peers and adults. Decision-making skills help them navigate complex social situations and academic tasks.

One of the first steps in recognizing socio-emotional factors is creating a safe and trusting classroom environment. Students need to feel secure and valued to engage fully in their learning. Teachers can foster this environment by showing genuine interest in their students' lives, listening actively, and responding empathetically. Building strong relationships with students can make a significant difference in their comfort level and willingness to participate in class.

Understanding the diverse backgrounds of students is another crucial aspect. Students may come from various cultural, socio-economic, and family environments, each bringing its own set of experiences and challenges. For instance, students from low-income families might face stressors such as food insecurity or unstable housing, which can affect their concentration and energy levels. Educators should be sensitive to these issues and provide support where possible, such as connecting families with community resources or offering flexible deadlines for assignments.

Trauma is a significant socio-emotional factor that can impact student learning. Students who have experienced trauma may exhibit a range of behaviors, from withdrawal and anxiety to aggression and defiance. Recognizing these behaviors as potential signs of trauma rather than misbehavior can shift the teacher's approach from punishment to support. Trauma-informed teaching practices involve creating a predictable and structured classroom environment, building strong relationships, and providing consistent emotional support.

Social dynamics within the classroom also play a crucial role. Bullying, exclusion, and peer pressure can significantly impact a student's emotional well-being and academic performance. Teachers can address these issues by fostering a culture of respect and inclusivity. Setting clear expectations for behavior, modeling respectful interactions, and addressing conflicts promptly and fairly can help create a positive social environment. Encouraging cooperative learning activities where students work together towards common goals can also enhance social skills and reduce negative behaviors.

Emotional intelligence (EI) is another important aspect of socio-emotional development. EI involves the ability to recognize, understand, and manage one's own emotions and the emotions of others. Teachers can help students develop EI by incorporating activities that promote self-awareness, empathy, and emotional regulation. For example, regular check-ins where students share how they are feeling can build self-awareness and empathy. Teaching mindfulness and relaxation techniques can help students manage stress and improve focus.

Another critical factor is the role of family in socio-emotional development. Engaging families in the educational process can provide valuable insights into students' socio-emotional needs and reinforce positive behaviors at home. Regular communication with parents and caregivers, through conferences, newsletters, or digital platforms, can build a strong partnership between home and school. Involving families in classroom activities and school events can also strengthen this connection and create a supportive community for students.

Peer relationships are central to socio-emotional development during school years. Friendships provide emotional support, opportunities for social learning, and a sense of belonging. However, not all students find it easy to form and maintain friendships. Teachers can facilitate positive peer interactions by creating opportunities for social engagement and teaching social skills explicitly. Activities such as group projects, peer mentoring, and social skill workshops can help students build and maintain healthy relationships.

Mental health is another critical aspect of socio-emotional well-being. Anxiety, depression, and other mental health issues can significantly affect a student's ability to concentrate, participate, and perform academically. Teachers should be aware of common signs of mental health issues, such as changes in behavior, mood, or academic performance. Providing a supportive environment where students feel comfortable seeking help is essential. Schools can also play a role by offering services such as counseling, mental health workshops, and resources for students and families.

Self-esteem and self-efficacy are key components of socio-emotional development that influence academic achievement. Students with high self-esteem and a strong sense of self-efficacy are more likely to take on challenges, persist through difficulties, and achieve their goals. Teachers can support the development of these traits by providing positive feedback, celebrating successes, and setting achievable goals. Encouraging a growth mindset, where students view effort and perseverance as paths to mastery, can also boost self-esteem and self-efficacy.

Social-emotional learning (SEL) programs are becoming increasingly popular in schools as a way to systematically address these factors. SEL programs typically include explicit instruction in skills such as emotional regulation, empathy, communication, and conflict resolution. These programs can be integrated into the curriculum through dedicated lessons, incorporated into daily routines, or infused into academic content. Research shows that SEL programs can improve not only socio-emotional skills but also academic performance, behavior, and attitudes toward school.

Assessing Academic Readiness

Understanding and assessing academic readiness is crucial for educators who aim to tailor instruction to meet the needs of each student. Academic readiness refers to the degree to which a student is prepared to engage with and benefit from the curriculum at a specific grade level. It encompasses a range of skills and knowledge, including cognitive abilities, prior knowledge, and socio-emotional factors. Effective assessment of academic readiness allows educators to identify students' strengths and weaknesses, enabling them to provide appropriate support and interventions.

One of the first steps in assessing academic readiness is to gather comprehensive information about each student. This can be achieved through a combination of formal assessments, teacher observations, and input from parents and previous teachers. Standardized tests, while sometimes controversial, can provide valuable data on students' proficiency in key areas such as reading, writing, and mathematics. These tests offer a snapshot of a student's current level of performance relative to grade-level expectations.

However, standardized tests should not be the sole measure of academic readiness. They often fail to capture the full range of a student's abilities and potential. For a more holistic understanding, teachers should incorporate formative assessments into their practice. These assessments, which can include quizzes, writing assignments, and classroom activities, provide ongoing insights into students' progress and areas needing improvement. Formative assessments are particularly useful because they allow for timely feedback and adjustment of instructional strategies.

Teacher observations play a vital role in assessing academic readiness. By closely monitoring students during classroom activities, teachers can gain insights into their engagement, problem-solving skills, and social interactions. For example, a student who consistently participates in class discussions and asks thoughtful questions may demonstrate a high level of intellectual curiosity and readiness for more challenging material. Conversely, a student who struggles to stay focused or complete tasks may need additional support to develop the skills required for academic success.

Input from parents and previous teachers can also provide valuable context. Parents often have a deep understanding of their child's strengths, interests, and challenges. Regular communication with parents can reveal important information about a student's learning experiences outside of school, such as participation in extracurricular activities, hobbies, and family dynamics. Previous teachers can offer insights based on their experiences with the student, highlighting areas of growth and identifying strategies that have been effective in the past.

In addition to academic skills, socio-emotional factors significantly influence academic readiness. A student's ability to manage emotions, build relationships, and cope with stress can impact their learning experience. For instance, a student with strong self-regulation skills is more likely to stay focused during lessons and complete assignments on time. Teachers can assess socio-emotional readiness through observations, discussions with students, and collaboration with school counselors. Activities that promote self-awareness and emotional regulation, such as mindfulness exercises and social-emotional learning (SEL) programs, can enhance students' readiness for academic challenges.

Assessing prior knowledge is another critical component of determining academic readiness. Students enter the classroom with varying levels of background knowledge and experiences that influence their ability to grasp new concepts. Diagnostic assessments, such as pre-tests or concept maps, can help teachers identify gaps in students' understanding and tailor instruction accordingly. For example, a diagnostic assessment in mathematics might reveal that a student understands basic arithmetic but struggles with more complex operations, indicating a need for targeted support in specific areas.

One effective approach to assessing academic readiness is through the use of performance-based assessments. These assessments require students to apply their knowledge and skills to real-world tasks, providing a more authentic measure of their abilities. For example, a science project that involves designing an experiment and analyzing data can reveal a student's understanding of scientific principles and their ability to think critically and solve problems. Performance-based assessments not only assess academic readiness but also promote deeper learning and engagement.

Another important consideration is the role of differentiated instruction in addressing varying levels of academic readiness. Differentiation involves tailoring instruction to meet the diverse needs of students, providing multiple pathways to learning. This can include offering different levels of challenge within the same lesson, providing additional support or enrichment activities, and using flexible grouping strategies. For instance, a teacher might use leveled reading groups to ensure that all students are working with texts that match their reading abilities, while also providing opportunities for peer collaboration and discussion.

Technology can also support the assessment of academic readiness. Digital tools and platforms offer a range of assessment options, from interactive quizzes and games to adaptive learning software that adjusts to a student's level of proficiency. These tools can provide immediate feedback and data that help teachers monitor progress and identify areas where students may need additional support. However, it is important to use technology thoughtfully and in conjunction with other assessment methods to ensure a comprehensive understanding of each student's readiness.

Incorporating student self-assessment and reflection into the process can empower students to take ownership of their learning. Encouraging students to set goals, monitor their progress, and reflect on their strengths and challenges can foster a growth mindset and increase motivation. For example, a student might keep a learning journal where they track their achievements and areas for improvement, setting specific goals for the next assessment period. This practice not only supports academic readiness but also helps students develop important skills for lifelong learning.

Ultimately, assessing academic readiness is an ongoing and dynamic process. It requires a combination of measures and a holistic approach that considers the whole child. By gathering comprehensive information from multiple sources, teachers can create a detailed picture of each student's readiness and provide the necessary support to ensure their success. This process involves collaboration with colleagues, parents, and students themselves, fostering a community of learners who are prepared to meet academic challenges with confidence and resilience.

Tailoring Instruction to Individual Needs

Every student enters the classroom with a unique set of skills, experiences, and learning preferences. Tailoring instruction to meet these individual needs is essential for creating an inclusive and effective learning environment. When teachers recognize and respond to the diverse needs of their students, they not only enhance academic outcomes but also foster a sense of belonging and engagement that motivates students to achieve their full potential.

One of the most effective ways to tailor instruction is through differentiated instruction. Differentiation involves adjusting the content, process, product, and learning environment based on students' readiness, interests, and learning profiles. This approach ensures that all students, regardless of their starting point, have access to meaningful learning experiences.

Understanding students' readiness levels is the first step in differentiation. Readiness refers to a student's current level of knowledge and skill in relation to the learning objectives. Pre-assessment tools, such as diagnostic tests or informal quizzes, can help teachers gauge students' understanding before beginning a new unit. For example, before starting a unit on fractions, a teacher might use a quick assessment to determine which students already have a solid grasp of basic fraction concepts and which students need more foundational support. Based on these results, the teacher can group students for targeted instruction, ensuring that each student receives the appropriate level of challenge and support.

Another critical aspect of differentiation is addressing students' interests. When students see a connection between their personal interests and the curriculum, their motivation and engagement increase. Teachers can gather information about students' interests through surveys, discussions, and observations. Incorporating student interests into lessons can be as simple as using examples from their favorite sports or hobbies in math problems or allowing them to choose research topics that excite them. For instance, if a student is passionate about space, a teacher might incorporate astronomy-related content into a science lesson, thus sparking the student's curiosity and enthusiasm.

Learning profiles, which encompass students' preferred learning styles and modalities, also play a significant role in differentiation. Some students may prefer visual learning, while others might excel through auditory or kinesthetic methods. Teachers can identify these preferences through learning style inventories or by observing how students interact with different types of materials and activities. Once learning profiles are understood, teachers can offer a variety of instructional approaches to accommodate different styles. For example, a teacher might use visual aids, such as charts and diagrams, for visual learners, while incorporating hands-on activities for kinesthetic learners.

Flexible grouping is a powerful strategy for differentiation. Instead of static ability groups, flexible grouping allows students to work with different peers depending on the task or objective. This approach prevents students from being labeled by their perceived abilities and provides opportunities for collaborative learning. For instance, a teacher might group students homogeneously for skill-based instruction in reading but heterogeneously for a project-based learning activity. This way, students can benefit from peer support and diverse perspectives, enhancing their learning experience.

Another key element in tailoring instruction is providing multiple pathways for students to demonstrate their understanding. Traditional assessments, such as tests and quizzes, may not capture the full range of students' abilities and knowledge. Offering varied assessment options, such as projects, presentations, or portfolios, allows students to showcase their learning in ways that align with their strengths. For example, a student who struggles with written tests might excel in a project where they can build a model or create a multimedia presentation. By giving students choices in how they demonstrate their learning, teachers can obtain a more accurate picture of their progress and abilities.

Technology can be a valuable tool in differentiating instruction. Digital platforms and resources offer a wealth of opportunities for personalized learning. Adaptive learning software, for example, adjusts the level of difficulty based on students' performance, providing immediate feedback and targeted practice. Online resources, such as educational videos and interactive simulations, can cater to different learning styles and interests. Moreover, technology allows for greater flexibility in how students access and engage with the curriculum. For instance, students with reading difficulties might benefit from text-to-speech tools, while those who are advanced can explore enrichment activities at their own pace.

Creating a supportive learning environment is also crucial for meeting individual needs. This involves establishing a classroom culture where all students feel valued and respected. Teachers can foster such an environment by setting clear expectations, modeling positive behaviors, and encouraging a growth mindset. When students believe that their abilities can improve with effort and perseverance, they are more likely to take on challenges and persist through difficulties. Additionally, providing opportunities for student voice and choice in the classroom helps build a sense of ownership and autonomy over their learning.

Scaffolding is another essential technique for supporting diverse learners. Scaffolding involves breaking down complex tasks into manageable steps and providing temporary support to help students achieve independence. This support can take various forms, such as graphic organizers, sentence starters, or guided practice. As students gain confidence and competence, the scaffolds are gradually removed, allowing them to take more responsibility for their learning. For example, in a writing assignment, a teacher might initially provide a detailed outline to help students organize their thoughts. Over time, the teacher can reduce the amount of guidance, encouraging students to create their own outlines.

Peer tutoring and cooperative learning are effective strategies for leveraging the strengths of individual students. In peer tutoring, students who have mastered certain skills or concepts can help their classmates who are struggling. This not only reinforces the tutor's knowledge but also provides personalized support for the tutee. Cooperative learning, where students work together in small groups to achieve common goals, promotes collaboration and communication skills. Assigning roles within the group, such as facilitator, recorder, or timekeeper, ensures that all students are actively engaged and contributing to the task.

Ongoing assessment and reflection are vital components of tailoring instruction. Formative assessments, such as exit tickets, think-pair-share activities, or learning logs, provide real-time insights into students' understanding and progress. These assessments help teachers identify who needs additional support and who is ready for more advanced challenges. Regular reflection, both by teachers and students, allows for continuous improvement and adjustment of instructional strategies. For instance, after a lesson, a teacher might reflect on what worked well and what could be improved, while students might reflect on their own learning and set goals for the future.

Incorporating students' cultural backgrounds and experiences into the curriculum is another important aspect of differentiation. Culturally responsive teaching recognizes and values the diverse cultural identities of students, creating a more inclusive and relevant learning experience. Teachers can achieve this by integrating culturally diverse materials, perspectives, and examples into their lessons. For example, in a history lesson, a teacher might include narratives and contributions from different cultural groups, ensuring that all students see themselves represented in the curriculum.

Creating an Inclusive Classroom Environment

Creating an inclusive classroom environment is both a fundamental necessity and an ongoing journey. It ensures that every student, regardless of background, ability, or learning style, feels welcomed, valued, and supported. The foundation of an inclusive classroom lies in the teacher's commitment to recognizing and celebrating diversity while fostering a sense of belonging among all students.

To start, understanding and embracing diversity is crucial. This encompasses not only cultural and linguistic differences but also variations in learning styles, abilities, and socio-economic backgrounds. Teachers must develop cultural competence, which involves being aware of their own cultural biases and learning about their students' cultures and experiences. This can be achieved through professional development, reading, and open conversations with students and their families. For instance, hosting a cultural heritage day where students share their customs and traditions can help build mutual respect and understanding.

Building strong relationships with students is another cornerstone of an inclusive classroom. When students feel that their teacher genuinely cares about them, they are more likely to engage and participate. Simple actions, such as greeting students at the door, taking an interest in their lives outside of school, and providing positive reinforcement, can make a significant difference. For example, a teacher might start each day with a brief check-in, asking students how they are feeling and if they have anything they would like to share. This practice not only builds rapport but also helps the teacher identify any potential issues that might affect a student's learning.

Creating a safe and supportive physical environment is also essential. The classroom should be arranged in a way that promotes accessibility and collaboration. Desks can be organized into clusters to facilitate group work and discussion, and spaces should be left clear for students who use wheelchairs or other mobility aids. Additionally, displaying diverse materials, such as books, posters, and resources that reflect various cultures and identities, helps students see themselves represented in the classroom. For example, a classroom library that includes books by authors from different backgrounds and stories featuring diverse characters can encourage students to explore and appreciate different perspectives.

Instructional strategies play a pivotal role in fostering inclusivity. Differentiated instruction, which involves tailoring teaching methods and materials to meet the diverse needs of students, is vital. This can include providing multiple means of representation, engagement, and expression. For instance, a teacher might present information through a combination of lectures, visual aids, and hands-on activities to cater to different learning styles. Additionally, offering students choices in how they demonstrate their understanding, such as through written reports, presentations, or creative projects, allows them to leverage their strengths.

Universal Design for Learning (UDL) is another effective approach. UDL principles emphasize providing all students with equal opportunities to learn by proactively designing lessons that accommodate varied needs. This involves creating flexible learning environments that can be adjusted to remove barriers. For example, a teacher might use captioned videos to support students with hearing impairments and provide digital texts that can be customized with larger fonts for students with visual impairments.

Classroom management policies should also reflect inclusivity. Establishing clear, consistent, and fair expectations for behavior helps create a predictable and safe environment. Involving students in creating these rules can foster a sense of ownership and accountability. For instance, a teacher might facilitate a class discussion where students collaboratively develop a code of conduct, emphasizing values such as respect, kindness, and cooperation. Additionally, implementing restorative practices, which focus on repairing harm and restoring relationships rather than punitive measures, can help address conflicts and build a positive classroom community.

An inclusive classroom also requires ongoing reflection and adaptation. Teachers must continuously assess the effectiveness of their strategies and seek feedback from students. This might involve regular check-ins, surveys, or reflective journals where students can share their thoughts and experiences. For example, a teacher might ask students to complete an anonymous survey at the end of each term, providing insights into what is working well and what could be improved. This feedback can then inform adjustments to teaching practices and classroom policies.

Collaboration with colleagues and families is another critical component. Working with other educators, such as special education teachers, counselors, and language specialists, can provide valuable support and resources. Regular communication with parents and caregivers, through conferences, newsletters, or digital platforms, helps build a strong partnership and ensures that everyone is working towards the same goals. For instance, a teacher might hold regular meetings with a special education teacher to discuss strategies for supporting students with learning disabilities and share progress updates with parents.

Promoting social-emotional learning (SEL) is also essential for an inclusive environment. SEL focuses on developing skills such as empathy, self-awareness, and relationship-building, which are crucial for creating a supportive and respectful classroom culture. Teachers can integrate SEL into their daily routines through activities such as class meetings, mindfulness exercises, and collaborative projects. For example, starting the day with a mindfulness activity, such as deep breathing or guided imagery, can help students regulate their emotions and prepare for learning.

Another powerful tool for fostering inclusivity is student voice. Giving students opportunities to express their opinions, make choices, and take on leadership roles empowers them and reinforces their sense of belonging. This can be achieved through student councils, class projects, or simply by encouraging students to share their ideas during lessons. For instance, a teacher might create a suggestion box where students can anonymously submit ideas for improving the classroom environment or propose topics they would like to explore.

Finally, celebrating successes and milestones, both big and small, helps build a positive and inclusive classroom culture. Recognizing students' achievements, whether academic or personal, reinforces their efforts and contributions. This can be done through verbal praise, certificates, or class celebrations. For example, a teacher might hold a monthly "achievement assembly" where students are recognized for their accomplishments in areas such as academics, behavior, or community service.

Chapter 2

Effective Teaching Strategies

Active Learning Techniques

Active learning techniques are essential for creating an engaging and effective educational environment. These methods shift the focus from passive reception of information to active participation, encouraging students to take ownership of their learning. Implementing active learning strategies can transform a classroom into a dynamic space where students are more involved, motivated, and better able to retain and apply knowledge.

One of the most effective active learning techniques is collaborative learning. This strategy involves students working together in small groups to solve problems, complete projects, or discuss concepts. Collaborative learning not only helps students develop a deeper understanding of the material but also enhances their communication, teamwork, and critical thinking skills. For example, a teacher might assign a group project on a historical event, where each student is responsible for researching and presenting a different aspect of the event. This approach ensures that students are actively engaged and learn from one another.

Think-pair-share is another powerful technique. In this method, the teacher poses a question or problem to the class, and students first think about their response individually. They then pair up with a partner to discuss their ideas before sharing with the larger group. This process allows students to refine their thoughts and gain new perspectives from their peers. For instance, in a science class, a teacher might ask students to think about the potential impacts of climate change, discuss their ideas with a partner, and then share their conclusions with the class. This technique not only encourages active participation but also helps students develop their verbal communication skills.

Active learning can also be fostered through problem-based learning (PBL). In PBL, students are presented with a real-world problem and must work to develop a solution. This method promotes critical thinking, creativity, and application of knowledge. For example, in a mathematics class, students might be given a scenario where they must create a budget for a community event. They would need to apply their mathematical skills to calculate costs, allocate resources, and ensure the budget is balanced. By working on realistic problems, students see the relevance of their learning and are more motivated to engage deeply with the material.

Another engaging technique is the use of case studies. Case studies provide detailed scenarios that require students to analyze information, make decisions, and justify their reasoning. This method is especially effective in fields such as business, law, and medicine but can be adapted to various subjects. For example, a teacher in a social studies class might present a case study of a historical conflict, asking students to examine the causes, stakeholders, and potential resolutions. Through this process, students develop analytical and decision-making skills that are crucial for their future careers.

Role-playing is an active learning technique that can make lessons more memorable and impactful. By assuming different roles, students can explore various perspectives and practice empathy. For instance, in an English literature class, students might role-play characters from a novel, acting out scenes and discussing motivations and conflicts. This approach helps students develop a deeper understanding of the characters and themes while improving their public speaking and improvisation skills.

Incorporating technology can also enhance active learning. Tools such as interactive simulations, educational games, and online discussion forums provide opportunities for students to engage with content in innovative ways. For example, a teacher might use a simulation to demonstrate complex scientific concepts, allowing students to manipulate variables and observe outcomes in real-time. Educational games can make learning fun and competitive, motivating students to achieve their best.

Flipped classrooms are another effective active learning strategy. In a flipped classroom, traditional lecture content is delivered outside of class, often through video lectures or readings, while class time is devoted to interactive activities and discussions. This approach allows students to learn at their own pace and come to class prepared to engage actively with the material. For instance, in a history class, students might watch a documentary about a historical event at home and then participate in a debate or group discussion during class. This method maximizes the use of class time for deeper learning and application.

Peer teaching is a technique where students take on the role of the teacher, explaining concepts to their classmates. This method reinforces the student's understanding and builds confidence while benefiting the entire class. For example, a teacher might assign each student a different topic to research and present to the class. This approach not only diversifies the learning experience but also encourages students to take responsibility for their learning.

Active learning also involves frequent formative assessments, such as quizzes, polls, and one-minute papers, which provide immediate feedback to both students and teachers. These assessments help identify areas where students are struggling and allow for timely interventions. For instance, a teacher might use an online polling tool to gauge students' understanding of a concept during a lesson, adjusting the instruction based on the results.

Incorporating movement into lessons is another way to promote active learning. Kinesthetic activities, such as moving to different stations, participating in hands-on experiments, or even simple stretching breaks, can enhance student engagement and improve concentration. For example, in a biology class, students might rotate through different lab stations to conduct experiments on various aspects of cellular biology. This approach keeps students physically active and mentally alert.

Active learning techniques also emphasize the importance of reflection. Encouraging students to reflect on their learning experiences helps them develop metacognitive skills and a deeper understanding of the material. Reflection can be facilitated through journals, discussion prompts, or self-assessment checklists. For instance, at the end of a project, a teacher might ask students to write a reflection on what they learned, what challenges they faced, and how they overcame them. This practice helps students internalize their learning and recognize their progress.

Storytelling can be a powerful active learning tool. By connecting lessons to real-life stories, teachers can make content more relatable and memorable. For example, in a geography class, a teacher might share stories of explorers and adventurers to illustrate the challenges and discoveries of different regions. This technique captures students' imaginations and helps them see the relevance of their studies.

Active learning requires a classroom culture that values curiosity, risk-taking, and collaboration. Teachers should create an environment where students feel safe to express their ideas, ask questions, and make mistakes. Building this culture involves establishing clear expectations, modeling active engagement, and providing positive reinforcement. For instance, a teacher might praise a student for asking a thoughtful question or taking a creative approach to a problem, reinforcing the value of active participation.

Differentiated Instruction

Differentiated instruction is a teaching philosophy centered around adapting educational methods to accommodate the diverse needs, skills, and interests of students. This approach recognizes that students learn in different ways and at varying paces, and it seeks to provide multiple pathways for students to engage with the material and demonstrate their understanding. By incorporating differentiated instruction, teachers can create a more inclusive and effective learning environment.

One foundational aspect of differentiated instruction is knowing your students. This involves understanding their backgrounds, learning preferences, strengths, and areas for growth. Teachers can gather this information through various means such as surveys, learning style assessments, and one-on-one conversations. For instance, a teacher might discover that some students are visual learners who benefit from diagrams and videos, while others are kinesthetic learners who need hands-on activities to grasp concepts. Armed with this knowledge, teachers can tailor their instructional strategies to meet the diverse needs of their students.

Curriculum modification is a key element of differentiated instruction. This can involve altering the content, process, product, or learning environment to better suit the needs of individual students. Content differentiation might involve providing materials at varying levels of difficulty or presenting information in different formats. For example, in a literature class, a teacher might offer a choice of books that vary in complexity, allowing students to select one that matches their reading level. Similarly, process differentiation could involve varying the types of activities students engage in to learn the material. A science teacher, for example, might offer lab experiments, virtual simulations, and research projects as different ways to explore a scientific concept.

Product differentiation is another powerful tool. This involves allowing students to demonstrate their learning in different ways. Instead of a one-size-fits-all approach, students might be given the option to write an essay, create a video, build a model, or present a skit. For instance, in a history class studying the Industrial Revolution, a student might choose to write a traditional research paper, while another might create a documentary or design a diorama depicting a factory. By providing various options, teachers can tap into students' strengths and interests, making learning more engaging and meaningful.

Flexible grouping is an essential strategy in differentiated instruction. This involves grouping students in different ways depending on the activity and learning objectives. Groups can be formed based on similar abilities, mixed abilities, interests, or learning preferences. For example, during a math lesson, a teacher might create small groups of students who need additional support with a concept, while other groups work on more advanced problems. These groups are not static and can change as students' needs and the learning goals evolve.

Ongoing assessment is crucial for effective differentiation. Formative assessments help teachers monitor student progress and adjust their instruction accordingly. These assessments can take many forms, such as quizzes, observations, discussions, and exit tickets. For example, a teacher might use a quick quiz at the end of a lesson to gauge understanding and identify students who need further support. Similarly, during a class discussion, the teacher can listen for misconceptions and provide immediate feedback. This continuous cycle of assessment and adjustment ensures that instruction is responsive to students' needs.

Another important aspect of differentiated instruction is providing appropriate levels of challenge and support. This means setting high expectations for all students while offering the necessary scaffolding to help them succeed.

Scaffolding can include strategies like providing graphic organizers, offering step-by-step instructions, or giving students sentence starters. For example, in a writing class, a teacher might provide struggling students with an outline template to help them organize their thoughts, while more advanced students are encouraged to develop their outlines independently. As students gain proficiency, the level of support can be gradually reduced, fostering greater independence.

Technology can be a valuable ally in differentiated instruction. Digital tools and resources offer a wide range of options for customizing instruction. Educational software can provide personalized practice based on students' skill levels, while online platforms can offer a variety of multimedia resources to cater to different learning styles. For instance, a math teacher might use an adaptive learning program that adjusts the difficulty of problems based on the student's performance, ensuring each student is working at an appropriate level of challenge. Additionally, technology can facilitate collaboration and communication, allowing students to work together on projects and share their learning in innovative ways.

Differentiated instruction also involves creating a supportive and inclusive classroom environment. This means fostering a culture of respect and collaboration, where all students feel valued and capable of success. Teachers can promote this environment by using positive reinforcement, celebrating diverse talents and achievements, and encouraging a growth mindset. For example, a teacher might praise a student for their effort and perseverance, rather than just their final product, reinforcing the idea that learning is a process. Group activities and peer tutoring can also help build a sense of community, as students learn to support and learn from one another.

Professional development is essential for teachers to effectively implement differentiated instruction. This might involve attending workshops, participating in study groups, or collaborating with colleagues to share strategies and resources. For instance, a school might organize a series of professional development sessions focused on differentiation techniques, where teachers can learn from experts and each other. Ongoing professional development helps teachers stay informed about best practices and continuously refine their skills.

Parental involvement is another critical component. Keeping parents informed and engaged in their child's learning can enhance the effectiveness of differentiated instruction. Regular communication through newsletters, conferences, and digital platforms allows parents to understand the strategies being used and how they can support their child's learning at home. For example, a teacher might send home a weekly update outlining the differentiated activities planned for the week, along with suggestions for how parents can reinforce these concepts through everyday activities.

Reflection is a vital part of the differentiation process. Teachers should regularly reflect on their instructional practices and consider what is working well and what could be improved. This might involve self-assessment, gathering feedback from students, or reviewing student performance data. For instance, after trying a new differentiation strategy, a teacher might ask students to complete a survey about their experience and use this feedback to make adjustments. Reflection helps teachers become more effective and responsive to their students' needs.

The ultimate goal of differentiated instruction is to help all students achieve their full potential. By recognizing and addressing the diverse needs of learners, teachers can create a more equitable and engaging educational experience. Differentiation is not about individualizing every lesson for every student but rather about providing a range of options and supports that allow each student to succeed. This approach requires flexibility, creativity, and a deep commitment to student-centered learning.

Implementing Technology in Education

Integrating technology into education can transform how students learn and how teachers facilitate learning. It is not merely about using the latest gadgets and apps, but about thoughtfully incorporating tools that enhance the educational experience, making learning more engaging, interactive, and personalized.

One of the first steps in implementing technology in education is to assess the current technological landscape of the school. This includes evaluating the availability of devices, internet connectivity, and the technical skills of both teachers and students. For example, a school might have a computer lab, but if the computers are outdated or the internet connection is unreliable, the potential benefits of using technology are limited. Similarly, if teachers and students are not comfortable using digital tools, professional development and training become essential.

Professional development is crucial for successful technology integration. Teachers need to be confident and competent in using new tools to effectively incorporate them into their teaching. This can involve workshops, online courses, and peer mentoring. For instance, a teacher who is proficient in using interactive whiteboards might lead a workshop for colleagues, demonstrating how to create engaging lessons that utilize this technology. Ongoing support is also important, as technology continually evolves and new tools become available.

Choosing the right technology tools is another critical step. This requires a thorough understanding of the educational goals and how technology can support them. For instance, if the goal is to improve student collaboration, tools like Google Classroom or Microsoft Teams might be appropriate. These platforms allow students to work together on projects, share resources, and communicate effectively. On the other hand, if the aim is to enhance individualized learning, adaptive learning software that adjusts the difficulty of tasks based on student performance could be beneficial. An example of this is Khan Academy, which provides personalized learning experiences in various subjects.

Implementing technology also involves rethinking traditional teaching methods. This might mean moving away from a lecture-based approach to a more student-centered model. Flipped classrooms are a popular method where students watch instructional videos at home and use class time for collaborative activities and hands-on learning. For example, a science teacher might assign a video on the theory of evolution for homework, and then use class time to conduct experiments or group discussions that deepen understanding.

Creating a supportive learning environment is essential when integrating technology. This includes not only the physical setup—such as having enough outlets and a reliable Wi-Fi network—but also fostering a culture that embraces experimentation and learning from failure. Students should feel comfortable exploring new tools without fear of making mistakes. Teachers can model this mindset by sharing their own learning experiences and encouraging a growth mindset.

One significant advantage of technology in education is the ability to provide immediate feedback. Digital tools can offer instant assessments, allowing students to see where they need to improve and giving teachers valuable insights into student progress. For instance, using a tool like Quizizz or Kahoot!, teachers can create interactive quizzes that provide real-time feedback. This not only makes learning more engaging but also helps identify areas where students may need additional support.

Technology can also facilitate differentiated instruction, catering to the diverse needs of students. Digital tools can offer a range of resources at different levels of difficulty, ensuring that all students are challenged appropriately. For example, in a reading lesson, a teacher might use an eBook platform that offers books at various reading levels, allowing each student to choose a text that matches their ability. Additionally, tools like speech-to-text and text-to-speech can support students with learning disabilities, making content more accessible.

Promoting digital literacy is another important aspect of integrating technology in education. Students need to learn not only how to use technology but also how to use it responsibly and ethically. This includes understanding online safety, recognizing credible sources, and using digital tools to create rather than just consume content. Teachers can incorporate lessons on digital citizenship into their curriculum, helping students navigate the digital world safely and responsibly.

Parental involvement is crucial in the successful implementation of technology in education. Keeping parents informed and engaged can enhance the learning experience and provide additional support for students at home. Schools can use digital communication tools to keep parents updated on their child's progress and any new technological initiatives. For example, a school might use a platform like ClassDojo to share updates, post assignments, and communicate with parents, creating a strong home-school connection.

One of the most exciting aspects of incorporating technology into education is the potential for global collaboration. Digital tools can connect students with peers, experts, and resources from around the world, broadening their perspectives and enhancing their learning experiences. For example, a social studies class might participate in a virtual exchange program, collaborating on projects with students in another country. This not only enhances their understanding of global issues but also develops important skills like communication and cultural awareness.

However, it is important to recognize and address the challenges that come with integrating technology in education. Issues such as digital equity and access must be considered to ensure that all students benefit from technological advancements. Schools need to develop strategies to support students who may not have access to devices or the internet at home. This might involve providing loaner devices, creating Wi-Fi hotspots, or partnering with community organizations to bridge the digital divide.

Evaluating the impact of technology on learning outcomes is essential to ensure that it is being used effectively. This involves collecting and analyzing data on student performance, engagement, and satisfaction. For instance, a school might use standardized test scores, surveys, and classroom observations to assess the impact of a new digital tool. Based on the findings, adjustments can be made to improve implementation and maximize the benefits.

Cooperative Learning and Group Work

Cooperative learning and group work are powerful pedagogical strategies that can transform classroom dynamics and improve student outcomes. When implemented effectively, these approaches foster collaboration, communication, and critical thinking, while also helping students develop social skills and a sense of community.

The foundation of cooperative learning lies in structuring activities that require students to work together towards a common goal. This involves more than just placing students in groups; it requires intentional planning and facilitation. A successful cooperative learning environment is built on the principles of positive interdependence, individual accountability, face-to-face promotive interaction, social skills, and group processing.

Positive interdependence is the cornerstone of cooperative learning. It means that each member of the group relies on and is essential to the success of the group. Tasks should be designed so that students understand their contributions are crucial. For instance, in a science project, one student might be responsible for researching the topic, another for conducting experiments, another for analyzing data, and another for presenting the findings. Each role is vital, and the absence of one member's input affects the entire project.

Individual accountability ensures that each student is responsible for their own learning and contributions. This can be achieved through assessments that evaluate both the group's work and individual performance. For example, after a group discussion, students might take a quiz individually to demonstrate their understanding of the topic. This encourages all members to participate actively and discourages free-riding.

Face-to-face promotive interaction involves students engaging directly with one another, discussing concepts, debating ideas, and providing feedback. This interaction helps deepen understanding and allows students to practice communication skills. Teachers can facilitate this by arranging the classroom to promote eye contact and conversation, and by encouraging students to explain their reasoning and listen to others.

Developing social skills is an integral part of cooperative learning. Working in groups requires students to practice skills such as leadership, decision-making, trust-building, and conflict resolution. Teachers can support this by explicitly teaching these skills and providing opportunities for students to practice them. For example, role-playing exercises can help students navigate conflicts and develop strategies for effective teamwork.

Group processing involves reflecting on the group's performance and identifying areas for improvement. After completing a group task, students should discuss what went well and what could be improved. This reflection helps groups become more effective over time and fosters a culture of continuous improvement. Teachers can guide this process by providing structured reflection activities and encouraging honest, constructive feedback.

One effective strategy for implementing cooperative learning is the use of structured group activities. These can include techniques like Think-Pair-Share, Jigsaw, and Group Investigation. Think-Pair-Share involves students thinking about a question individually, discussing their thoughts with a partner, and then sharing their insights with the larger group. This technique encourages all students to participate and helps them articulate their ideas.

The Jigsaw method involves dividing a topic into segments, with each group member responsible for learning and teaching one segment to the others.

This not only promotes individual accountability but also ensures that everyone contributes to the group's understanding. For example, in a history lesson, one student might research the causes of a conflict, another the key events, another the consequences, and another the perspectives of different stakeholders.

Group Investigation is a more open-ended approach where students work together to explore a topic of interest. They formulate questions, conduct research, and present their findings. This method encourages higher-order thinking and allows students to take ownership of their learning. For instance, in a literature class, students might investigate the themes of a novel and present their interpretations through a multimedia project.

To ensure the success of cooperative learning, teachers need to create a supportive classroom environment. This includes establishing clear expectations, providing ongoing support, and fostering a culture of respect and collaboration. Clear expectations help students understand their roles and responsibilities, and ongoing support ensures they have the resources and guidance they need to succeed.

Teachers can support cooperative learning by providing scaffolding and resources. Scaffolding involves breaking tasks into manageable steps and providing support at each stage. For example, when introducing group work, a teacher might start with simple tasks and gradually increase complexity as students become more comfortable with the process. Providing resources such as graphic organizers, checklists, and rubrics can also help students stay organized and focused.

Fostering a culture of respect and collaboration is crucial for cooperative learning. This involves creating an inclusive classroom environment where all students feel valued and respected. Teachers can model respectful behavior, set ground rules for group interactions, and address any conflicts or issues that arise promptly and fairly. Encouraging students to appreciate diverse perspectives and strengths can also enhance group dynamics.

One of the challenges of cooperative learning is managing group dynamics and ensuring equitable participation. Teachers need to be proactive in monitoring groups and intervening when necessary. This might involve rotating group roles, using peer evaluations, and providing feedback on group processes. For instance, if one student tends to dominate discussions, the teacher might assign them a different role that requires listening and summarizing others' contributions.

Assessing cooperative learning can also be challenging, as it involves evaluating both the group's work and individual contributions. Teachers can use a combination of formative and summative assessments to gauge student learning and group effectiveness. Formative assessments might include observation, self-assessments, and peer feedback, while summative assessments could involve group projects, presentations, and individual quizzes or tests.

Incorporating technology can enhance cooperative learning by providing tools for communication, collaboration, and creativity. Online platforms such as Google Docs, Padlet, and Slack allow students to collaborate in real time, share resources, and provide feedback. These tools can also help teachers monitor progress and provide support. For example, in a group writing project, students can use Google Docs to draft, edit, and comment on each other's work, while the teacher provides guidance and feedback.

Ultimately, the goal of cooperative learning and group work is to prepare students for the collaborative nature of the real world. By working together, students learn to appreciate diverse perspectives, communicate effectively, and solve complex problems. These skills are essential for success in college, careers, and beyond.

Formative and Summative Assessments

Assessments are fundamental to the educational process, serving as critical tools for measuring student learning, guiding instructional decisions, and providing feedback. Among the various types of assessments, formative and summative assessments are the most widely used and offer distinct yet complementary benefits.

Formative assessments are ongoing processes that provide immediate feedback to both students and teachers about learning progress. These assessments are typically informal and can take many forms, such as quizzes, observations, class discussions, and homework assignments. The primary goal of formative assessments is to gather information that can be used to improve teaching and learning in real-time. For instance, a teacher might use a quick exit ticket at the end of a lesson to gauge students' understanding of the material covered. If the majority of students struggle with a particular concept, the teacher can adjust the next day's lesson to address the confusion.

One effective formative assessment technique is the use of questioning strategies during class discussions. Open-ended questions encourage students to think critically and express their understanding in their own words. For example, in a history class, a teacher might ask, "How do you think the Industrial Revolution changed everyday life for people?" This type of question prompts students to analyze and synthesize information rather than simply recalling facts. The teacher can then listen to the responses to assess comprehension and probe deeper if necessary.

Another valuable formative assessment tool is peer assessment. When students evaluate each other's work, they engage in reflective thinking and gain insights from their peers' perspectives. This process can be structured through rubrics that outline specific criteria for evaluation. For instance, in a writing class, students might use a rubric to provide feedback on each other's essays, focusing on aspects such as clarity, organization, and argument strength. This not only helps the writer improve but also reinforces the evaluator's understanding of good writing practices.

Formative assessments also play a crucial role in differentiating instruction. By identifying individual students' strengths and weaknesses, teachers can tailor their instruction to meet diverse needs. For example, if a math teacher notices that some students are struggling with fractions while others have mastered the concept, they can create small groups for targeted instruction. One group might work on foundational skills with the teacher, while another group tackles more advanced problems independently. This ensures that all students receive the appropriate level of challenge and support.

Summative assessments, on the other hand, are typically administered at the end of an instructional period to evaluate overall student learning. These assessments are often formal and standardized, such as final exams, standardized tests, and end-of-term projects. The primary purpose of summative assessments is to determine whether students have achieved the learning objectives and to provide a measure of accountability for both students and educators.

One of the most common forms of summative assessment is the multiple-choice test. These tests are efficient for assessing a broad range of knowledge and skills and can be scored quickly and objectively. However, they often fail to capture deeper understanding and critical thinking. To address this limitation, teachers can incorporate a variety of question types, such as short answer and essay questions, which require students to explain their reasoning and demonstrate higher-order thinking.

Performance-based assessments are another powerful form of summative assessment. These assessments require students to apply their knowledge and skills in real-world contexts, providing a more comprehensive picture of their learning. For example, in a science class, a summative assessment might involve designing and conducting an experiment, analyzing the results, and presenting the findings in a written report. This type of assessment not only evaluates students' scientific knowledge but also their ability to think critically, solve problems, and communicate effectively.

Portfolios are a unique form of summative assessment that allows for a holistic evaluation of student learning over time. A portfolio is a collection of student work that demonstrates growth, achievement, and reflection. For instance, in an art class, a portfolio might include sketches, completed projects, and written reflections on the creative process. Portfolios provide a rich, nuanced view of student learning and can be particularly valuable for assessing skills that develop gradually, such as writing or artistic ability.

Both formative and summative assessments have their strengths and limitations, and the most effective assessment systems integrate both types. Formative assessments provide ongoing feedback that can inform instruction and support student learning throughout the process. Summative assessments, meanwhile, offer a final measure of achievement and accountability. Together, they create a comprehensive assessment framework that supports both teaching and learning.

To implement effective formative and summative assessments, teachers must be intentional in their planning and use a variety of assessment methods. This requires a deep understanding of the learning objectives and the ability to design assessments that align with those objectives. For instance, if a learning objective focuses on critical thinking, a teacher might use formative assessments that involve analysis and synthesis tasks, such as debates or case studies. For the summative assessment, the teacher might design a project that requires students to apply their critical thinking skills to a real-world problem.

Feedback is a crucial component of both formative and summative assessments. For formative assessments, feedback should be timely, specific, and actionable, helping students understand their progress and how to improve. For example, instead of simply marking an answer as incorrect, a teacher might provide a hint or ask a probing question that guides the student to the correct answer. In summative assessments, feedback can help students understand their overall performance and identify areas for future growth. For instance, after grading a final exam, a teacher might provide a summary of common mistakes and offer suggestions for improvement.

Assessment data should also be used to inform instructional decisions and improve teaching practices. Teachers can analyze assessment results to identify trends and patterns, such as common misconceptions or areas where students consistently struggle. This information can guide curriculum adjustments, targeted interventions, and professional development. For example, if assessment data reveals that students are struggling with a particular math concept, the teacher might seek out additional resources or training to better address that concept in future lessons.

Incorporating technology can enhance both formative and summative assessments. Digital tools such as online quizzes, interactive simulations, and e-portfolios provide new ways to assess student learning and offer immediate feedback. These tools can also facilitate data collection and analysis, allowing teachers to track student progress more efficiently. For example, an online quiz platform might provide detailed reports on student performance, highlighting areas of strength and weakness.

Ultimately, the goal of formative and summative assessments is to support student learning and development. By using a combination of assessment methods, providing meaningful feedback, and using assessment data to inform instruction, teachers can create a dynamic and responsive learning environment. This comprehensive approach to assessment not only measures student achievement but also promotes continuous growth and improvement.

Chapter 3

Building Engagement through Curriculum Design

Designing Engaging Lesson Plans

Designing engaging lesson plans is both an art and a science, requiring creativity, careful planning, and a deep understanding of students' needs and learning styles. An effective lesson plan not only conveys information but also inspires and motivates students, making learning an active and joyful process. The foundation of a successful lesson plan is clear objectives. Understanding what you want your students to learn by the end of the lesson is crucial. These objectives should be specific, measurable, achievable, relevant, and time-bound (SMART). For instance, instead of setting a vague goal like "understand photosynthesis," a SMART objective would be "explain the process of photosynthesis and identify the role of chlorophyll in converting sunlight into chemical energy by the end of the lesson."

Once the objectives are set, the next step is to consider the students' prior knowledge and readiness. Gauging where your students currently stand allows you to build on their existing knowledge and address any gaps. This can be achieved through pre-assessment activities, such as quick quizzes, class discussions, or concept maps. For example, if you're teaching a lesson on fractions, you might start with a few problems to see how comfortable students are with basic fraction concepts.

Engaging lesson plans often start with a compelling hook to capture students' interest. This could be a surprising fact, a provocative question, a short video clip, or a hands-on activity. Imagine starting a lesson on ancient Egypt by showing a clip of the discovery of King Tutankhamun's tomb. This not only grabs attention but also sets the stage for deeper exploration into the topic.

Variety is key to maintaining engagement throughout the lesson. Incorporating different types of activities caters to various learning styles and keeps students involved. Visual learners benefit from diagrams, charts, and videos, while auditory learners might prefer lectures and discussions. Kinesthetic learners, on the other hand, engage more with hands-on activities and experiments. For instance, in a science lesson about the water cycle, you might include a mix of activities: watching a video, creating a water cycle diagram, and conducting an experiment demonstrating evaporation and condensation.

Interactive activities are particularly effective in engaging students. Group work, peer teaching, and collaborative projects encourage active participation and deeper understanding. In a history lesson on the American Revolution, you could divide the class into groups, each representing a different perspective (e.g., Patriots, Loyalists, British soldiers), and have them debate the causes and consequences of the revolution. This not only makes the lesson more dynamic but also helps students understand the complexity of historical events.

Incorporating technology can also enhance engagement. Tools like interactive whiteboards, educational apps, and online simulations provide new ways to present material and engage students. For instance, in a math lesson on geometry, using an interactive app to manipulate shapes and explore their properties can make abstract concepts more concrete and understandable.

A well-designed lesson plan also includes opportunities for formative assessment. These are brief, informal checks for understanding that provide immediate feedback to both the teacher and the students. Techniques like thumbs up/thumbs down, exit tickets, or quick write-ups help gauge whether students are grasping the material and allow for adjustments on the fly. For example, after teaching a concept, you might ask students to write a one-minute summary of what they've learned and any questions they still have. This not only reinforces the material but also highlights areas that might need further clarification.

Differentiation is another crucial aspect of an engaging lesson plan. Recognizing that students have diverse needs and abilities, and adapting instruction accordingly, ensures that all students can access the material and achieve the objectives. This might involve providing different levels of reading materials, offering choices in how students demonstrate their understanding, or using flexible grouping strategies. For example, in a literature lesson, you might offer a range of books at varying reading levels and allow students to choose one that interests them and matches their reading ability.

Closure is an often-overlooked but essential component of a lesson plan. It provides a way to wrap up the lesson, reinforce key points, and connect the day's learning to future lessons. This could be a brief summary, a reflective discussion, or a quick activity that ties everything together. For instance, at the end of a lesson on ecosystems, you might have students draw a concept map linking different components of an ecosystem and explaining how they interact.

Reflecting on the lesson after it has been taught is also a valuable practice. Consider what worked well, what didn't, and how the lesson could be improved. Gathering feedback from students can provide insights into their experiences and help refine future lessons. This might involve asking students to complete a brief survey or having a class discussion about the lesson's strengths and areas for improvement.

Incorporating storytelling into lesson plans can significantly enhance engagement. Stories have the power to make abstract concepts relatable and memorable. For example, when teaching about the civil rights movement, sharing personal stories of individuals who lived through that period can bring the history to life and foster a deeper emotional connection. Similarly, in a science lesson about the solar system, telling the story of the Voyager missions can ignite curiosity and wonder about space exploration.

Creating a positive and inclusive classroom environment is also essential for keeping students engaged. Establishing clear expectations, fostering mutual respect, and encouraging a growth mindset help students feel safe and motivated to participate. Building strong relationships with students, showing genuine interest in their lives, and celebrating their successes, however small, can make a big difference in their engagement and learning.

The physical setup of the classroom can also impact engagement. Arranging desks in a way that facilitates interaction, creating learning stations with different activities, and displaying student work can make the classroom a more inviting and stimulating place. For instance, setting up a reading corner with comfortable seating and a variety of books can encourage more independent reading and exploration.

Professional development and collaboration with colleagues are valuable resources for designing engaging lesson plans. Sharing ideas, observing each other's teaching, and participating in workshops or training sessions can provide fresh perspectives and new strategies. For example, planning lessons with a team of teachers can lead to more innovative and effective approaches, such as cross-curricular projects that integrate multiple subjects into a cohesive learning experience.

Ultimately, the goal of a lesson plan is not just to cover the curriculum but to inspire a love of learning and foster critical thinking skills. By setting clear objectives, considering students' prior knowledge, using a variety of engaging activities, incorporating technology, providing opportunities for assessment, differentiating instruction, and reflecting on the lesson, teachers can create dynamic and effective lesson plans that captivate students' interest and support their academic growth.

Incorporating Real-World Applications

Bridging the gap between classroom learning and real-world applications can transform the educational experience, making it more relevant, engaging, and impactful for students. By demonstrating how academic concepts apply in everyday life, teachers can ignite students' curiosity and motivation, fostering a deeper understanding and appreciation of the subject matter.

One effective approach to incorporating real-world applications is through project-based learning (PBL). This method involves students working on a project over an extended period, which requires them to apply knowledge and skills from various disciplines to solve a real-world problem or answer a complex question. For instance, a science class might engage in a project to design and build a sustainable garden. Students would need to research plant biology, understand environmental science, apply mathematical skills for planning and measurements, and perhaps even explore historical agricultural practices. This hands-on experience encourages collaboration, critical thinking, and creativity, as students see the tangible results of their efforts.

Connecting lessons to students' everyday lives also enhances their relevance. When students can relate what they are learning to their own experiences, they are more likely to be engaged and retain the information. For example, in a math class, teaching concepts like budgeting or interest rates can be tied to personal finance. Students could create a budget for a hypothetical event or calculate the interest on a savings account, making abstract concepts more concrete and practical.

Guest speakers and field trips are powerful tools for bringing real-world applications into the classroom. Inviting professionals from various fields to speak to students can provide insights into how academic subjects are used in different careers. A visit from an engineer, for instance, can show students how physics and math are essential in designing and building structures. Field trips offer immersive experiences where students can see firsthand how their learning applies outside the classroom. A visit to a science museum, a historical site, or a local business can provide rich, contextual learning experiences that textbooks alone cannot offer.

Another strategy is integrating current events into the curriculum. Using news articles, documentaries, and discussions about ongoing global or local issues can make lessons more dynamic and relevant. For instance, a social studies class could examine the impact of climate change by analyzing recent weather patterns, reading about policy responses, and discussing the science behind climate models. This approach not only deepens students' understanding of the subject but also helps them develop critical thinking skills as they evaluate different sources and perspectives.

Service learning is an educational approach that combines community service with academic learning objectives. By participating in service projects, students can apply classroom knowledge to address real community needs. For example, a biology class might partner with a local environmental organization to conduct a habitat restoration project. Students would gain hands-on experience in ecology and environmental science while contributing positively to their community. This approach fosters a sense of civic responsibility and helps students see the broader impact of their education.

Incorporating technology can also bridge the gap between classroom learning and real-world applications. Digital tools and platforms offer a wealth of resources and opportunities for students to engage with real-world data and simulations. For example, students can use online databases to access and analyze scientific data, participate in virtual lab experiments, or collaborate with peers from around the world on global projects. These experiences not only enhance technical skills but also prepare students for the increasingly digital and interconnected world.

Role-playing and simulations are engaging methods to bring real-world scenarios into the classroom. By simulating real-life situations, students can explore complex concepts and practice problem-solving in a controlled environment. For instance, a government class might simulate a legislative session where students take on the roles of lawmakers, debating and voting on proposed bills. This hands-on approach helps students understand the intricacies of political processes and the importance of civic engagement.

Interdisciplinary teaching is another effective way to connect classroom learning with real-world applications. By integrating subjects such as math, science, history, and language arts, teachers can create a more holistic and relevant learning experience. For instance, a unit on the industrial revolution could include lessons on the historical context, the scientific advancements of the time, the mathematical principles behind the machinery, and the literature that reflects the societal changes. This approach not only enriches students' understanding but also highlights the interconnectedness of knowledge and its application in the real world.

Encouraging students to pursue independent research projects on topics of personal interest can also foster real-world connections. Allowing students to explore areas they are passionate about and guiding them through the research process can lead to deeper engagement and understanding. For example, a student interested in medicine might research a particular disease, its treatment options, and the latest advancements in medical technology. This self-directed learning approach empowers students to take ownership of their education and see how their academic pursuits can lead to real-world impact.

Collaborating with local businesses and organizations can provide students with practical experiences and insights into various industries. Partnerships with businesses can lead to internships, job shadowing opportunities, and real-world projects that give students a taste of professional life. For instance, a technology class might partner with a local software company to develop a new app, providing students with hands-on experience in coding, project management, and teamwork. These experiences not only enhance learning but also help students build valuable skills and networks for their future careers.

Reflective practice is an essential component of incorporating real-world applications into education. Encouraging students to reflect on their learning experiences helps them make connections between classroom knowledge and real-world contexts. Reflective activities, such as journaling, group discussions, or presentations, allow students to articulate what they have learned, how they applied it, and what impact it has on their understanding of the world. This metacognitive process deepens learning and helps students internalize the relevance of their education.

Incorporating real-world applications in education is not just about making learning more interesting; it's about preparing students for life beyond the classroom. When students see the connections between what they are learning and the world around them, they are more likely to be motivated, engaged, and successful. This approach helps develop critical thinking, problem-solving, and collaboration skills that are essential for personal and professional success.

Using Project-Based Learning

Project-based learning (PBL) is an educational approach that transforms the traditional classroom dynamic by engaging students in real-world problems and projects. This method emphasizes active exploration and hands-on experiences, encouraging students to take responsibility for their learning and develop essential skills such as critical thinking, collaboration, and creativity.

Imagine a high school biology class tasked with designing an urban garden. The project begins with students researching the benefits of urban gardens, understanding plant biology, and exploring sustainable practices. They must then plan and execute the garden, considering factors such as soil quality, sunlight, and water needs. Throughout this process, students apply their knowledge from various disciplines—biology, environmental science, mathematics, and even art—to create a functional and aesthetically pleasing garden.

One of the key benefits of PBL is its ability to make learning more relevant and engaging. When students see the direct application of their studies to real-world situations, their motivation and interest levels soar. Instead of learning isolated facts and concepts, students understand how their knowledge can solve problems and make a difference. This connection to real-life scenarios fosters a deeper understanding and retention of the material.

PBL also promotes the development of essential 21st-century skills. In the urban garden project, for example, students must work together to plan, implement, and maintain the garden. This collaboration requires effective communication, conflict resolution, and teamwork. Students also develop problem-solving skills as they troubleshoot issues such as pest control or plant diseases. Additionally, managing the project's timeline and resources cultivates organizational and time-management skills, which are invaluable in both academic and professional settings.

To implement PBL effectively, teachers need to design projects that are meaningful, challenging, and aligned with learning objectives. A well-crafted project should have a clear purpose and relevance to the students' lives or communities. It should also be complex enough to require critical thinking and problem-solving but still achievable within the given timeframe and resources.

Assessment in PBL can be multifaceted, incorporating both formative and summative evaluations. Formative assessments, such as regular check-ins, peer reviews, and self-assessments, provide ongoing feedback and help students stay on track. Summative assessments might include a final presentation, a written report, or a tangible product like the urban garden. These assessments should measure not only the final outcome but also the process, including collaboration, research, and problem-solving skills.

A crucial aspect of successful PBL is fostering a supportive and collaborative classroom environment. Teachers play the role of facilitators rather than traditional instructors, guiding students through their projects and providing the necessary resources and support. This shift in the teacher's role encourages students to take ownership of their learning and develop independence.

Consider a middle school history class undertaking a project on local history. Students might start by researching significant events and figures from their community's past. They could then create a multimedia presentation or a documentary, interviewing local historians and residents, and visiting historical sites. This project not only deepens students' understanding of history but also connects them to their community and enhances their research, communication, and technological skills.

While PBL can be highly effective, it also presents challenges. Designing meaningful projects that align with curriculum standards and learning objectives requires careful planning and creativity. Teachers must also manage the logistics of project work, ensuring that all students are engaged and making progress. Additionally, assessing PBL can be more complex than traditional tests and quizzes, requiring comprehensive rubrics and multiple forms of evaluation.

Despite these challenges, the benefits of PBL make it a worthwhile endeavor. By engaging students in meaningful projects, teachers can create a more dynamic and relevant educational experience. PBL not only enhances academic understanding but also prepares students for the complexities of the real world by developing critical thinking, collaboration, and problem-solving skills.

For instance, in a high school economics class, students might be tasked with creating a business plan for a small startup. This project would require them to research market trends, understand financial principles, and develop marketing strategies. Students would need to collaborate, delegate tasks, and present their business plan to a panel of judges, simulating a real-world entrepreneurial experience. This type of project not only reinforces economic concepts but also provides practical skills that students can apply in their future careers.

Incorporating technology into PBL can further enhance its effectiveness. Digital tools and platforms can facilitate research, collaboration, and presentation. For example, students can use online databases to gather information, collaborative software to work together on documents, and multimedia tools to create engaging presentations. Technology can also provide access to a broader range of resources and experts, enriching the learning experience.

Reflecting on the learning process is another important component of PBL. Encouraging students to reflect on their experiences helps them consolidate their learning and understand the broader implications of their work. Reflection can take many forms, including journals, group discussions, or individual presentations. By reflecting on what they learned, how they worked together, and what they might do differently next time, students develop a deeper understanding of both the content and the skills they have acquired.

Imagine an elementary school class working on a project about renewable energy. Students could start by researching different types of renewable energy sources, such as solar, wind, and hydroelectric power. They might then build models or simulations to demonstrate how these energy sources work. Finally, they could present their findings to the school community, advocating for renewable energy initiatives. This project not only teaches scientific principles but also fosters public speaking, advocacy, and environmental stewardship.

PBL can also be tailored to individual student interests and strengths, making learning more personalized and inclusive. By allowing students to choose aspects of the project that align with their passions, teachers can boost engagement and motivation. For example, in a literature class, students might work on a project where they create their own adaptations of classic novels. Some students might focus on writing, while others might create illustrations, videos, or even stage performances. This flexibility allows students to showcase their unique talents and learn in ways that resonate with them.

Effective communication with parents and the broader community is essential for the success of PBL. Keeping parents informed about the projects and their objectives helps garner support and involvement. Community partnerships can also enhance projects by providing resources, expertise, and real-world connections. For instance, local businesses, museums, or non-profit organizations might collaborate with schools on PBL initiatives, providing students with valuable insights and opportunities.

Integrating Cross-Curricular Connections

When considering the integration of cross-curricular connections in education, it's essential to understand the profound impact this approach can have on student learning and development. Cross-curricular connections involve the blending of different subject areas to create a more cohesive and comprehensive learning experience. This method not only enhances students' understanding of individual subjects but also helps them see the interrelationships between different domains of knowledge, fostering a more holistic educational experience.

Think of a classroom where a history lesson on the Industrial Revolution seamlessly incorporates elements of science, technology, and literature. Students might begin by examining the historical events and figures that shaped the era. They could then delve into the technological advancements and scientific discoveries of the time, understanding how innovations in machinery and industry transformed societies. Finally, they might read literary works from the period, gaining insight into how these changes influenced the lives and thoughts of people. This interconnected approach not only enriches the learning experience but also helps students develop a deeper and more nuanced understanding of the subject matter.

One of the primary advantages of integrating cross-curricular connections is the promotion of critical thinking and problem-solving skills. When students are encouraged to draw connections between different subjects, they learn to approach problems from multiple perspectives. This interdisciplinary thinking mirrors real-world scenarios where issues are rarely confined to a single domain. For example, addressing climate change requires knowledge of environmental science, economics, political science, and ethics. By practicing cross-curricular connections, students are better prepared to tackle complex problems with a more comprehensive toolkit.

Moreover, cross-curricular connections can make learning more engaging and relevant. When students see how their studies apply to real-world contexts, their motivation and interest often increase. For instance, a project that combines math and art by having students create geometric designs can make abstract mathematical concepts more tangible and enjoyable. Similarly, integrating social studies with current events can help students understand the relevance of historical knowledge in today's world, fostering a greater appreciation for the subject.

To effectively integrate cross-curricular connections, teachers can start by identifying natural overlaps between subjects. This process often begins with collaborative planning among educators from different disciplines. By discussing their curricula and identifying common themes or topics, teachers can design lessons and projects that bridge multiple subjects. For example, a unit on ancient civilizations in a history class could be paired with lessons on ancient engineering and architecture in a science class, as well as studies of mythology in a literature class. This collaborative approach ensures that the connections are meaningful and well-integrated rather than forced or superficial.

Assessment in a cross-curricular framework can also be multifaceted. Instead of traditional tests that focus on isolated facts, assessments can include projects, presentations, and portfolios that reflect students' ability to synthesize information from different subjects. For instance, a student might create a multimedia presentation that combines historical research with artistic expression, demonstrating their understanding of both history and art. This type of assessment not only evaluates students' knowledge but also their ability to apply and integrate that knowledge in creative and meaningful ways.

Consider a middle school project where students explore the concept of sustainability. This project could encompass science lessons on ecosystems and renewable energy, social studies discussions on the impact of human activity on the environment, and math exercises calculating carbon footprints and resource consumption. Students might then present their findings through a combination of written reports, visual displays, and digital media, showcasing their interdisciplinary understanding of sustainability. Such a project not only deepens students' knowledge but also empowers them to think critically about their role in promoting a sustainable future.

Teachers can also leverage technology to facilitate cross-curricular connections. Digital tools and resources can provide access to a wealth of interdisciplinary content and foster collaboration among students. For example, online platforms can enable students to work together on projects, share resources, and provide feedback, regardless of their physical location. Additionally, multimedia tools can help students create dynamic presentations that integrate text, images, videos, and interactive elements, enhancing their ability to communicate complex ideas.

Reflective practices are another vital component of integrating cross-curricular connections. Encouraging students to reflect on their learning experiences helps them internalize the connections they have made and understand their broader implications. Reflection can take various forms, such as journals, discussions, or self-assessment exercises. Through reflection, students can articulate how the integration of different subjects has enriched their understanding and consider how they might apply this interdisciplinary approach in future learning endeavors.

Imagine an elementary school project where students investigate the water cycle. This project could include science lessons on evaporation, condensation, and precipitation, geography lessons on the distribution of water resources around the world, and art activities creating visual representations of the water cycle. Students might also write stories or poems about the journey of a water droplet, integrating language arts into the project. By exploring the water cycle through multiple lenses, students gain a well-rounded understanding of the concept and develop an appreciation for the interconnectedness of natural systems.

It's important to recognize that integrating cross-curricular connections requires flexibility and creativity from both teachers and students. Traditional classroom structures and schedules may need to be adapted to allow for interdisciplinary projects and activities. This might involve block scheduling, where longer class periods enable more in-depth exploration of topics, or team-teaching arrangements where educators from different disciplines co-teach and collaborate on lessons. While these changes can present logistical challenges, the benefits of a more integrated and holistic learning experience are well worth the effort.

Parental and community involvement can also enhance the effectiveness of cross-curricular connections. By engaging parents and community members in interdisciplinary projects, schools can provide students with additional resources and perspectives. For example, inviting guest speakers from various professions can help students see how different fields intersect in the real world. Community partnerships can also offer opportunities for students to apply their interdisciplinary learning in practical settings, such as internships, service projects, or local research initiatives.

Leveraging Student Interests

Education thrives when students are genuinely engaged, and one of the most effective ways to foster engagement is by leveraging student interests. This approach not only motivates students but also makes learning more meaningful and enjoyable. When students see the connection between their passions and their studies, they are more likely to invest effort and enthusiasm into their education.

Consider a high school student who is passionate about video games. Instead of viewing this interest as a distraction, educators can harness it to teach various subjects. For example, a math teacher might use game design to explain algebraic concepts, showing how algorithms and equations are fundamental to creating game mechanics. In a history class, the evolution of video gaming technology can be a springboard for discussions about technological advancements and their social impacts. By connecting academic content to a student's existing interests, teachers can transform potential disengagement into active participation.

Identifying student interests requires more than casual observation; it involves intentional dialogue and relationship-building. Teachers can start by creating an environment where students feel comfortable sharing their passions. Simple activities like interest inventories, surveys, or informal conversations can provide valuable insights. For instance, a middle school teacher might begin the school year with a questionnaire asking about students' hobbies, favorite subjects, and extracurricular activities. This information can then inform lesson planning, ensuring that content is relevant and engaging.

Incorporating student interests into the curriculum can take various forms, from small adjustments to full-scale project-based learning. For example, an English teacher might allow students to choose books for a reading assignment based on their personal preferences, whether they're drawn to fantasy, mystery, or historical fiction. This choice fosters a sense of ownership over their learning and can lead to richer, more enthusiastic literary discussions. Similarly, a science teacher might design experiments around topics that intrigue students, such as space exploration, environmental conservation, or robotics.

Project-based learning (PBL) is an excellent strategy for leveraging student interests. PBL involves students in complex, real-world projects that require sustained inquiry and collaboration. By aligning these projects with students' passions, teachers can create powerful learning experiences. Imagine a classroom where students interested in environmental issues work on a project to design a sustainable garden for their school. This project could encompass lessons in biology, chemistry, and environmental science, as well as math skills for budgeting and design. The students' intrinsic motivation to address an issue they care about can drive deeper engagement and more meaningful learning.

Another example might involve students passionate about social justice working on a project to raise awareness about a particular issue within their community. This could include researching the history and current state of the issue, creating informative materials, and organizing events or campaigns. Through this project, students would not only learn about social studies and civics but also develop skills in research, communication, and advocacy. By connecting academic content to real-world issues that matter to students, educators can make learning more relevant and impactful.

Technology can also play a crucial role in leveraging student interests. Digital tools and platforms offer endless possibilities for customizing learning experiences. For instance, students interested in music might use software to compose and produce their own pieces, learning about the physics of sound, mathematical patterns in music, and the cultural contexts of different musical genres. Those fascinated by coding can engage in programming projects that teach logical thinking, problem-solving, and creativity.

While integrating student interests into the curriculum is essential, it is equally important to balance this with the need to cover required standards and objectives. Teachers can achieve this balance by identifying key learning goals and then finding creative ways to relate them to students' passions. For example, a history teacher might need to cover the Industrial Revolution but can do so through the lens of students' interests in technology, engineering, or even fashion. By framing mandatory content in ways that resonate with students, educators can maintain academic rigor while enhancing engagement.

Involving students in the planning process can also be beneficial. When students have a say in what and how they learn, they are more likely to be invested in their education. This might involve co-creating project ideas, choosing topics for research, or even helping to design assessments. For example, a teacher might present a broad topic, such as "renewable energy," and then work with students to narrow it down to specific areas of interest, such as solar power, wind energy, or electric vehicles. This collaborative approach not only leverages student interests but also empowers them to take ownership of their learning.

It's also important to recognize that student interests can evolve over time. What captivates a student's attention in September might be different by March. Therefore, teachers should remain flexible and open to adjusting their approaches as needed. Regular check-ins, reflections, and feedback sessions can help educators stay attuned to students' changing interests and adapt their strategies accordingly.

Consider a scenario where a student who initially expressed a strong interest in sports becomes increasingly fascinated by photography. A responsive teacher might shift gears, incorporating photography into lessons that originally focused on sports. This could involve analyzing sports photography, exploring the physics of motion through camera techniques, or even creating a photojournalism project documenting local sports events. By staying adaptable, teachers can continue to engage students effectively, even as their interests shift.

Ultimately, leveraging student interests is about creating a learning environment that values and celebrates individuality. It requires teachers to be observant, empathetic, and innovative. By connecting academic content to the diverse passions of their students, educators can inspire a love of learning that extends beyond the classroom.

One memorable example comes from a high school science teacher who noticed a student's fascination with marine life. Recognizing this interest, the teacher designed a semester-long project focused on oceanography. The student conducted experiments on water salinity, researched marine ecosystems, and even organized a virtual presentation with a marine biologist. This personalized approach not only deepened the student's understanding of science but also ignited a lifelong passion for marine biology.

Leveraging student interests is not a one-size-fits-all approach; it requires ongoing effort and creativity. Teachers must continually seek ways to connect curriculum content with the varied and evolving interests of their students. By doing so, they can create a dynamic and engaging educational experience that motivates students to reach their full potential.

In classrooms where student interests are at the forefront, learning becomes more than just a series of tasks to complete. It transforms into a journey of discovery, curiosity, and passion. Students who see their interests reflected in their education are more likely to develop a positive attitude toward learning, exhibit higher levels of engagement, and achieve greater academic success.

Chapter 4

Creating a Positive Learning Environment

Building a Supportive Classroom Culture

Creating a supportive classroom culture is essential for the success and well-being of both students and teachers. It fosters an environment where students feel safe, valued, and motivated to learn. This chapter delves into practical strategies for building such a culture, combining empathy, structure, and creativity.

A supportive classroom culture begins with a strong foundation of mutual respect. As a teacher, setting the tone from the first day is crucial. Greet each student warmly and learn their names quickly. This simple act communicates that you see them as individuals and care about their presence. Establish clear expectations for behavior, emphasizing respect for everyone in the classroom. When students understand that their voices and identities are respected, they are more likely to respect others and contribute positively to the classroom environment.

Building relationships is at the heart of a supportive classroom culture. Take the time to get to know your students beyond their academic abilities. Engage in conversations about their interests, hobbies, and lives outside of school. Share appropriate aspects of your own life to create a sense of connection and trust. For example, if a student mentions they love soccer, ask about their favorite team or how their last game went. These small interactions can significantly strengthen the student-teacher bond.

A classroom culture that celebrates diversity and inclusion is also crucial. Acknowledge and honor the different backgrounds, cultures, and experiences that students bring to the classroom. Incorporate diverse perspectives into your curriculum and discussions. For instance, when teaching literature, select texts from a variety of authors representing different cultures and viewpoints. Create opportunities for students to share their own stories and experiences, fostering a sense of belonging and validation.

Active listening is another key component. When students feel heard, they are more likely to open up and engage. Practice active listening by maintaining eye contact, nodding, and providing feedback that shows you understand their points. Avoid interrupting or dismissing their contributions. When students share their thoughts, whether during a lesson or in a casual conversation, respond thoughtfully and considerately. This practice not only builds trust but also encourages students to participate more actively in class.

Consistent and fair discipline is vital for maintaining a supportive environment. Students need to know that there are clear and consistent consequences for their actions. However, it's important to approach discipline with empathy and understanding. When addressing behavioral issues, focus on the behavior rather than the student. Use restorative practices, such as discussing the impact of their actions and exploring ways to make amends, rather than solely punitive measures. This approach helps students learn from their mistakes and understand the importance of their behavior within the classroom community.

Creating a physically and emotionally safe space is paramount. Ensure that the classroom is a place where students feel secure and free from bullying or harassment. Establish and enforce a zero-tolerance policy for any form of bullying. Encourage students to report any incidents and take immediate action to address them. Additionally, provide resources and support for students who may be struggling with personal issues, whether academic, social, or emotional. Let students know that you are available to listen and help them find the support they need.

Fostering a growth mindset can also contribute significantly to a supportive classroom culture. Encourage students to view challenges and mistakes as opportunities for learning and growth. Praise effort and perseverance rather than innate ability. Share stories of individuals who achieved success through hard work and resilience. By promoting a growth mindset, you help students develop a positive attitude toward learning and build the confidence to tackle difficult tasks.

Collaboration and teamwork should be integral parts of the classroom experience. Design activities and projects that require students to work together, share ideas, and support one another. Group work not only enhances learning but also builds social skills and fosters a sense of community. Encourage students to appreciate each other's strengths and contributions. For example, in a science project, one student might excel at research while another is skilled in presenting findings. By working together, they can achieve a better result than they would individually.

Regularly reflecting on classroom dynamics and seeking student feedback can help maintain a supportive culture. Create opportunities for students to share their thoughts on the classroom environment and suggest improvements. This could be through anonymous surveys, suggestion boxes, or open discussions. Act on their feedback to show that you value their input and are committed to making the classroom a better place for everyone.

Recognizing and celebrating achievements, both big and small, can boost morale and motivation. Take the time to acknowledge students' efforts and successes, whether it's a high test score, improvement in a particular area, or acts of kindness. Celebrate these moments publicly to create a positive and encouraging atmosphere. This recognition can take various forms, such as verbal praise, certificates, or a class bulletin board showcasing student achievements.

Incorporating social-emotional learning (SEL) into the curriculum is another effective way to build a supportive classroom culture. SEL focuses on developing students' abilities to manage emotions, set goals, show empathy, maintain positive relationships, and make responsible decisions. Integrate SEL activities and discussions into your daily routines. For example, start the day with a check-in where students can share how they are feeling and any concerns they might have. Teach conflict resolution skills and provide opportunities for students to practice them in real-life situations.

Classroom rituals and routines can also contribute to a sense of stability and community. Establish routines that provide structure and predictability, helping students feel secure and focused. Begin and end each day with specific rituals, such as a morning meeting or a reflection circle, to build a sense of community and set a positive tone. These routines can reinforce the values and expectations of the classroom culture.

Empowering students by giving them responsibilities and leadership roles can enhance their sense of ownership and belonging. Assign classroom jobs or roles that allow students to contribute to the classroom community. Rotate these roles regularly so that every student has the opportunity to take on different responsibilities. Leadership roles can range from managing classroom materials to leading a group activity. When students feel that they have a stake in the classroom, they are more likely to take pride in their environment and support their peers.

Flexibility and adaptability are essential qualities for maintaining a supportive classroom culture. Be prepared to adjust your teaching strategies and plans based on the needs and dynamics of your students. Sometimes, unexpected events or issues may arise that require you to deviate from your planned lessons. Embrace these moments as opportunities to address students' immediate concerns and reinforce the supportive environment. For instance, if a significant event occurs in the community, take the time to discuss it and provide a space for students to express their feelings and thoughts.

Establishing Clear Expectations and Routines

Establishing clear expectations and routines is a cornerstone of effective teaching and classroom management. When students know what is expected of them and understand the daily structure, they are more likely to thrive academically and socially. This chapter will explore how to create and maintain these expectations and routines to foster a productive and positive learning environment.

One of the first steps in establishing clear expectations is setting the tone on the first day of school. From the moment students walk through the door, they need to understand the classroom rules and the reasons behind them. Begin by clearly explaining your expectations for behavior, work habits, and interactions. For example, you might state that respect is a fundamental rule in your classroom, emphasizing that it applies to how they treat their peers, the teacher, and even the classroom environment.

To make these expectations concrete, involve students in creating a classroom contract. This can be a collaborative activity where students contribute to and agree upon the rules. By taking part in this process, students are more likely to feel responsible for adhering to the agreed-upon standards. Write the final contract on a large poster and display it prominently in the classroom as a constant reminder.

Consistency is key when it comes to enforcing expectations. If rules are applied inconsistently, students may become confused or feel that certain behaviors are sometimes acceptable. To avoid this, respond to rule violations promptly and fairly. Use a calm and firm tone, explaining which expectation was not met and why it is important. This approach helps students understand the impact of their actions and the importance of maintaining a respectful and orderly environment.

Routines are equally important in creating a stable and predictable classroom environment. Establishing a daily schedule helps students know what to expect and reduces anxiety. Begin by outlining the structure of a typical day, including start times, subject transitions, break periods, and end-of-day procedures. For younger students, visual schedules can be particularly helpful. Use pictures and symbols to represent different activities, making it easier for them to follow along.

Morning routines set the tone for the entire day. Develop a consistent procedure for students to follow as soon as they enter the classroom. This might include hanging up their coats, submitting homework, and starting on a morning task such as journaling or silent reading. Such routines help students transition smoothly from home to school and prepare them mentally for the day ahead.

Transitions between activities can be challenging, but with clear routines, they can become seamless. Use signals or cues to indicate when it's time to switch tasks. For example, you might ring a bell, play a specific piece of music, or use a hand signal. Give students a few minutes' warning before the transition so they can begin to wrap up their current activity. Consistently using these signals helps students anticipate and prepare for changes, minimizing disruptions.

Classroom jobs are another effective way to establish routines and give students a sense of responsibility. Assigning roles such as line leader, materials manager, or board cleaner not only helps the classroom run smoothly but also fosters a sense of community. Rotate these jobs regularly so that every student gets the opportunity to take on different responsibilities. Clearly explain the duties associated with each role and hold students accountable for performing them well.

Homework routines are critical for reinforcing learning outside the classroom. Clearly communicate your expectations for homework, including how it should be recorded, completed, and submitted. Use a consistent format for assigning homework, such as a weekly packet or a daily log. Provide students with a quiet time during the day to write down their assignments and ask any questions. Reviewing homework together in class can also help reinforce the routines and ensure that students understand the material.

Behavior management routines are essential for maintaining a positive classroom environment. Develop a system for recognizing and rewarding positive behavior, such as a points system or a reward chart. Similarly, have a clear and consistent approach for addressing negative behavior. Explain the consequences of rule violations and apply them consistently. For example, you might use a warning system where students receive a verbal reminder first, followed by a loss of privileges if the behavior continues. The key is to be predictable and fair in your responses.

Communication with parents is an integral part of establishing clear expectations and routines. Regularly update parents on classroom rules, schedules, and their child's progress. Use tools such as newsletters, emails, or a class website to keep them informed. Encourage parents to reinforce classroom expectations at home and involve them in supporting their child's learning. When parents and teachers work together, students receive a consistent message about the importance of following expectations and routines.

Reflecting on and adjusting routines is necessary as the school year progresses. Solicit feedback from students about what is working and what might need improvement. Be open to making changes that enhance the classroom environment. For example, if students consistently struggle with a particular transition, brainstorm ways to make it smoother. Flexibility and willingness to adapt demonstrate to students that their input is valued and that routines are meant to support their success.

Modeling expected behaviors is one of the most powerful ways to teach students about expectations and routines. Demonstrate how to complete tasks, interact respectfully, and follow procedures. For instance, if you expect students to walk quietly in the hallway, practice this behavior with them and provide positive reinforcement when they do it correctly. Your actions set the standard for what is acceptable in the classroom.

Building a classroom community where students feel connected and responsible for each other can significantly enhance the effectiveness of expectations and routines. Encourage teamwork and collaboration through group projects and peer learning activities. Use class meetings to discuss challenges and celebrate successes. When students feel a sense of belonging and mutual responsibility, they are more likely to adhere to the established expectations and routines.

Incorporating technology can also support the establishment of clear expectations and routines. Utilize digital tools to organize assignments, track behavior, and communicate with students and parents. For example, a classroom management app can help you monitor student behavior and provide instant feedback. Online platforms can streamline homework submission and provide students with resources to support their learning. Embrace technology as a way to enhance, not replace, the personal connections and routines within the classroom.

Promoting Respect and Inclusivity

Respect and inclusivity are foundational principles for any thriving classroom. When students feel respected and included, they are more likely to engage, participate, and excel. Creating an environment where every student feels valued requires deliberate strategies and a commitment to fostering a culture of empathy and understanding.

One of the first steps in promoting respect and inclusivity is understanding the diverse backgrounds of your students. This includes their cultural, linguistic, and socio-economic backgrounds, as well as their individual learning styles and needs. Take the time to learn about your students through surveys, discussions, and observations. This knowledge will help you tailor your teaching methods to be more inclusive and relevant to each student.

Building relationships is crucial in fostering a respectful and inclusive classroom. Greet students warmly each day and show genuine interest in their lives. Ask about their interests, hobbies, and experiences. When students feel known and appreciated, they are more likely to respect their peers and contribute positively to the classroom community.

Modeling respectful behavior is essential. Demonstrate how to listen actively, speak kindly, and resolve conflicts peacefully. For instance, if a student interrupts another during a discussion, gently remind them of the importance of listening while others speak. Use phrases like, "Let's give everyone a chance to share their thoughts," to reinforce the value of respectful communication.

Establishing clear, consistent expectations for behavior is another key element. Develop a set of classroom rules that emphasize respect and inclusivity, such as "Treat others with kindness" and "Value everyone's contributions." Involve students in creating these rules to give them a sense of ownership and responsibility. Display the rules prominently in the classroom and refer to them regularly.

Incorporate activities that celebrate diversity and foster empathy. Use literature, videos, and guest speakers to expose students to different cultures, perspectives, and experiences. Organize events like cultural fairs or international days where students can share their heritage and learn about others. These activities help students appreciate diversity and understand the importance of inclusivity.

Group work is an effective way to promote respect and inclusivity. When students work together on projects, they learn to appreciate each other's strengths and perspectives. Assign diverse groups and rotate them regularly to ensure that students have the opportunity to collaborate with all their peers. Encourage group members to divide tasks equitably and support each other throughout the project.

Addressing bias and stereotypes is crucial in promoting an inclusive environment. Challenge any discriminatory remarks or behaviors immediately and use them as teaching moments. Educate students about the harmful effects of stereotypes and encourage them to think critically about their own biases. Activities like role-playing and discussions can help students understand the impact of bias and develop more inclusive attitudes.

Create a classroom environment that is physically and emotionally safe for all students. Arrange the classroom in a way that is accessible to students with different needs and abilities. Ensure that materials and resources reflect the diversity of the student body. For example, include books and posters that represent various cultures, languages, and family structures.

Encourage open dialogue and create opportunities for students to share their experiences and perspectives. Use discussion circles or forums where students can talk about issues related to respect and inclusivity. Establish ground rules for these discussions to ensure that they are respectful and constructive. For instance, you might agree that everyone should listen without interrupting and that all opinions are valid, even if they differ.

Implement restorative practices to address conflicts and build a sense of community. Restorative practices focus on repairing harm and restoring relationships rather than simply punishing misbehavior. When conflicts arise, facilitate a restorative circle where those involved can express their feelings, understand the impact of their actions, and agree on steps to make amends. This approach helps students learn from their mistakes and fosters a more supportive and respectful classroom environment.

Incorporate social-emotional learning (SEL) into your curriculum to help students develop skills like empathy, self-awareness, and relationship-building. SEL activities can include mindfulness exercises, role-playing scenarios, and reflective writing. These activities teach students how to manage their emotions, understand others' perspectives, and interact positively with their peers.

Involve parents and guardians in your efforts to promote respect and inclusivity. Communicate regularly with families about your classroom expectations and the importance of respect and inclusivity. Invite them to participate in classroom activities and events that celebrate diversity. Encourage parents to reinforce these values at home by modeling respectful behavior and discussing the importance of inclusivity with their children.

Provide professional development opportunities for yourself and your colleagues to learn more about promoting respect and inclusivity. Attend workshops, read relevant literature, and participate in discussions about best practices. Share what you learn with your colleagues and collaborate on strategies to create more inclusive classrooms.

Evaluate and reflect on your own practices regularly. Seek feedback from students, parents, and colleagues about the effectiveness of your efforts to promote respect and inclusivity. Use this feedback to make adjustments and improvements. Reflect on your own biases and how they might affect your teaching. Commit to continuous growth and learning in this area.

Recognize and celebrate the progress your students make in developing respect and inclusivity. Acknowledge acts of kindness, cooperation, and empathy. Use positive reinforcement to encourage these behaviors. Celebrate milestones and achievements that reflect the values of respect and inclusivity, such as successful group projects or thoughtful contributions to class discussions.

Managing Classroom Behavior

Effective classroom management is critical to creating an environment where students can focus on learning and personal growth. Managing classroom behavior involves establishing clear expectations, consistent routines, and strategies for addressing both positive and negative behaviors. This chapter explores practical and actionable advice for teachers to effectively manage classroom behavior, ensuring a conducive and respectful learning atmosphere.

Starting with the first day of school, it's crucial to set the tone for behavior expectations. Greet each student warmly and establish a welcoming atmosphere. Begin by introducing the classroom rules and procedures, explaining their importance for maintaining an orderly environment. Engage students in a discussion about why these rules matter, and how they contribute to a positive learning space. For example, you might explain that raising hands before speaking ensures everyone has a chance to be heard.

Consistency in enforcing rules is essential. If students perceive that rules are applied arbitrarily, it can lead to confusion and potential misbehavior. Make sure to apply consequences consistently and fairly, regardless of who the student is. When a rule is broken, address it immediately and calmly. For instance, if a student is talking out of turn, remind them of the rule and the reason behind it. Consistent enforcement helps students understand that the rules are important and that there are predictable consequences for breaking them.

Positive reinforcement is a powerful tool in managing classroom behavior. Recognize and reward positive behaviors to encourage their repetition. This can be done through verbal praise, reward systems, or privileges. For example, you might compliment a student who consistently completes their assignments on time or show appreciation for a student who helps a classmate. A reward system, such as earning points for good behavior that can be traded for small prizes or privileges, can motivate students to adhere to classroom expectations.

Building relationships with students is another key aspect of managing behavior. When students feel respected and valued, they are more likely to respect the classroom rules and the teacher. Take time to get to know your students individually. Learn about their interests, strengths, and challenges. Personal connections can make a significant difference in a student's behavior. For instance, knowing that a student loves soccer can help you engage them in conversations and use soccer-related examples in lessons, making them feel more connected and understood.

Clear and engaging instruction can prevent many behavioral issues. When students are actively engaged in their learning, they are less likely to become disruptive. Plan lessons that are interactive and cater to different learning styles. Use a variety of instructional strategies, such as group work, hands-on activities, and technology integration, to keep students interested and involved. A well-structured lesson with clear objectives and engaging activities helps minimize off-task behavior.

Transitions between activities can be moments of potential disruption. Establishing clear routines for transitions can help maintain order. Use signals, such as a bell or a hand signal, to indicate that it's time to move to the next activity. Give students a countdown or a few minutes' warning before transitioning, allowing them to finish their current task and prepare for the next. Practicing transitions at the beginning of the year can help students understand the expectations and move smoothly between activities.

Addressing misbehavior promptly and effectively is crucial. When a student exhibits disruptive behavior, it's important to remain calm and composed. Avoid escalating the situation by responding with anger or frustration. Instead, use a calm and firm tone to address the behavior. Describe the behavior you observed, explain why it's problematic, and state the consequence. For example, you might say, "I noticed you were talking while I was giving instructions. It's important to listen so everyone knows what to do. Since you were talking, you'll need to stay in for a few minutes of recess to review the instructions with me."

Restorative practices can be effective in managing classroom behavior and repairing relationships.

Instead of focusing solely on punishment, restorative practices involve the student in understanding the impact of their behavior and making amends. When a conflict arises, facilitate a restorative conversation where the involved parties can express their feelings, discuss the impact of the behavior, and agree on steps to repair the harm. This approach helps students develop empathy and take responsibility for their actions.

Proactive strategies can prevent many behavior issues before they start. Anticipate potential triggers and plan accordingly. For example, if you know that a particular student struggles with transitions, provide them with additional support, such as a visual schedule or a personal reminder. Create a classroom environment that minimizes distractions and supports focus. Ensure that materials are organized and easily accessible, and that the classroom layout promotes a positive learning atmosphere.

Involving students in the creation of classroom norms can increase their buy-in and cooperation. Facilitate a discussion where students can contribute ideas for classroom rules and expectations. This collaborative approach helps students feel a sense of ownership and responsibility for maintaining a positive classroom environment. When students help create the rules, they are more likely to follow them and hold each other accountable.

Communication with parents is an integral part of managing classroom behavior. Keep parents informed about their child's behavior, both positive and negative. Regular communication can help build a partnership with parents, allowing them to support behavior expectations at home. Use tools such as newsletters, emails, or a classroom website to provide updates and tips for reinforcing positive behavior. When parents and teachers work together, students receive consistent messages about behavior expectations.

Professional development can enhance your skills in managing classroom behavior. Attend workshops, read relevant books and articles, and participate in discussions with colleagues about effective behavior management strategies. Continuous learning and reflection can help you stay informed about new techniques and approaches, and improve your ability to manage behavior effectively.

Reflecting on your own practices is important for continuous improvement. Take time to evaluate what strategies are working well and what might need adjustment. Seek feedback from students and colleagues about your behavior management approach. Use this feedback to make informed changes and improve your effectiveness. Reflecting on your own experiences and learning from them can help you grow as an educator and create a more positive classroom environment.

Recognize that every student is unique, and what works for one may not work for another. Be flexible and willing to adapt your strategies to meet the needs of individual students. Some students may require additional support or different approaches to manage their behavior effectively. Be patient and persistent, and remember that building a positive classroom environment takes time and effort.

Encouraging Student Autonomy and Responsibility

Encouraging student autonomy and responsibility is pivotal in fostering a classroom environment where learners feel empowered and motivated. By promoting independence and a sense of accountability, students develop essential life skills that extend beyond academic success. This chapter delves into practical strategies and approaches for educators to effectively nurture autonomy and responsibility among students, creating a harmonious and dynamic learning environment.

One of the first steps in encouraging student autonomy is to provide choices within the classroom. Offering students options in their assignments, projects, and even seating arrangements can significantly boost their sense of control and ownership over their learning. For example, allowing students to choose between different topics for a research paper or giving them the freedom to select their partners for a group project can enhance their engagement and intrinsic motivation. When students are given the power to make decisions, they become more invested in the outcomes and take greater responsibility for their work.

Creating a classroom culture that values student voice is another essential component. Encourage students to express their opinions, ideas, and preferences openly. This can be achieved through regular class meetings where students can discuss classroom issues, suggest improvements, and share their thoughts on various topics. By actively listening to and considering student input, teachers demonstrate that they respect and value their students' perspectives. This inclusivity helps build a community of learners who feel confident in their ability to contribute meaningfully.

Setting clear expectations and goals is crucial in promoting responsibility. When students understand what is expected of them and what they are working towards, they are more likely to take ownership of their actions. Clearly defined objectives provide a roadmap for students, guiding their efforts and helping them stay focused. For instance, breaking down a larger project into smaller, manageable tasks with specific deadlines can help students plan and organize their work effectively. Providing rubrics and checklists can also aid students in self-monitoring their progress and ensuring they meet the set standards.

Encouraging self-assessment and reflection is a powerful way to foster autonomy and responsibility. Teach students to evaluate their own work and identify areas for improvement. This can be done through regular reflective journals, self-assessment checklists, or peer review sessions. When students take the time to reflect on their learning process and outcomes, they develop a deeper understanding of their strengths and weaknesses. This self-awareness is crucial for personal growth and encourages students to take responsibility for their learning journey.

Incorporating collaborative learning opportunities can also promote autonomy and responsibility. Group work and cooperative learning activities require students to share responsibility and hold each other accountable. When working in groups, students must communicate effectively, delegate tasks, and manage their time. This collaborative dynamic mirrors real-world situations where teamwork and shared responsibility are essential. By participating in group projects, students learn to trust their peers, rely on each other's strengths, and collectively achieve their goals.

Providing constructive feedback is vital in guiding students towards greater autonomy and responsibility. Feedback should be specific, actionable, and focused on improvement rather than criticism. For example, instead of simply pointing out errors, provide suggestions on how to correct them and encourage students to think critically about their mistakes. Engaging students in feedback discussions allows them to take an active role in their learning process. When students understand how to apply feedback to enhance their performance, they become more independent and accountable learners.

Fostering a growth mindset is another effective way to encourage autonomy and responsibility. Emphasize the importance of effort, perseverance, and learning from mistakes. Help students understand that intelligence and abilities can be developed through dedication and hard work. By praising effort rather than innate talent, teachers can motivate students to take risks and embrace challenges. This mindset shift empowers students to take control of their learning, view setbacks as opportunities for growth, and persist in the face of difficulties.

Modeling responsible behavior is essential for teaching students to be autonomous and accountable. Demonstrate punctuality, preparedness, and a positive attitude towards learning. Show students how to organize their materials, manage their time, and approach tasks systematically. When teachers exemplify these behaviors, students are more likely to emulate them. Additionally, sharing personal experiences of overcoming challenges and taking responsibility for mistakes can inspire students to adopt similar attitudes and behaviors.

Encouraging students to set their own goals is a powerful strategy for fostering autonomy and responsibility. Guide students in identifying short-term and long-term goals that are specific, measurable, achievable, relevant, and time-bound (SMART). Support them in developing action plans to achieve these goals, and regularly review their progress. When students set and work towards their own goals, they take ownership of their learning and become more motivated to succeed.

Creating a supportive and safe learning environment is crucial for promoting autonomy and responsibility. Ensure that students feel comfortable taking risks, asking questions, and seeking help when needed. Establish a classroom atmosphere where mistakes are viewed as learning opportunities rather than failures. Encourage a sense of community where students support and respect each other. When students feel safe and supported, they are more likely to take initiative and responsibility for their learning.

Incorporating technology can also enhance student autonomy and responsibility. Utilize digital tools and resources that allow students to explore topics independently, collaborate with peers, and manage their assignments. For example, online learning platforms can provide students with access to a wealth of information and interactive activities that cater to different learning styles. Digital tools such as project management apps can help students track their progress and stay organized. By integrating technology, teachers can create a more personalized and self-directed learning experience.

Encouraging students to take on leadership roles within the classroom can further promote autonomy and responsibility. Assigning roles such as group leader, class representative, or project manager allows students to practice decision-making, problem-solving, and organizational skills. Leadership opportunities help students build confidence, develop a sense of accountability, and learn to balance individual and group responsibilities. When students experience the responsibilities of leadership, they gain a deeper understanding of the importance of autonomy and accountability.

Finally, involving parents and guardians in the process can reinforce the development of autonomy and responsibility. Regular communication with families about student progress, goals, and areas for improvement helps create a supportive network for the student. Encourage parents to provide opportunities for their children to take responsibility at home, such as managing chores, organizing their study time, or making decisions about extracurricular activities. When students receive consistent messages about autonomy and responsibility from both school and home, they are more likely to internalize these values.